the process

emily schromm

Published by Emily Schromm.

Copyright © 2019 by Emily Schromm. All rights reserved of course.

Library of Congress Cataloging-In-Publication Data
The process / Emily Schromm
ISBN: 978-0-578-56901-7
WC: 14,060
1. Entrepreneurship. 2. Poetry. 3. Business. 4. Process. 5. Creativity.

Illustrations and Cover design by Hilary Thomas (@arktikos.book)
Formatted and edited in beautiful Central Oregon by Shawn Mihalik
Printed in the U.S.A.

contents

origin	2
do	16
feel	86
know	126
make	176
outro	234

To my mom
    who allows the universe to line up just right
    who yells "you're my champion" before I take flight
    who teaches me unconditional love time and time again
            through watching you, my true journey began

sketches done by Hilary Thomas
polar bear – KNOWER – friend for eternity

@arktikos.book

the process

ORIGIN

My name is Emily Schromm.
college drop-out. the chick from the real world. that girl from the challenge.
the next fitness star. fitness model. the one on instagram.
coach. nutritionist. meathead. hippie. Meathead Hippie.
founder of emfit – herbal element – the empack –
the body awareness project – platform strength.
entrepreneur and -

Hummingbird.
Witchy.
Empath.
Curious.
Creator.

I
Am
Emily
Schromm.

I ASSUME MANY ARE OPENING this book expecting something about nutrition or fitness, perhaps some workouts. That has been my world for the last 10 years: teaching others about eating enough protein and how taking a fish oil can help you heal.

It is strangely hard to re-birth into more of yourself.
I would assume it feels like the first time being birthed at all.

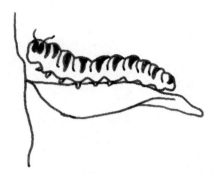

Do caterpillars know they will become butterflies?

I spend a lot of my time in my own head. Although my thinking has gotten me through many problems, there is a downside. Too much thinking with too little expression becomes the ticking time bomb of our anxiety and a type of crazy that effortlessly turns into loneliness if we don't name it fast enough.

I had always wanted to be the type of person who kept a journal. For as long as I can remember I would full-heartedly commit to writing in some form of a diary every morning or every night. I would be great at it for approximately two days, and on day three it was already forgotten about. Months later I would find them
tucked in random corners
filled with empty pages
holding them in my hand
as if I was holding another broken promise to myself.

During a recent move, I found 5 of these "START STOP"

journals. All were different styles and types: some fancier than others maybe thinking that if I paid more for them I would start to care. I knew writing was a release for me, not able to count the times I would pull my car over on the side of the road to let my body scream something out in random iPhone notes or scraps of paper. Writing poetry felt like peace, it felt like the gust of wind so desperately needed on a hot, sticky day. But this release was reactive, not preventative. I would always wait for an implosion before giving myself permission to do the very thing I knew would help.

As I stared at these 5 "start stop" journals, I went through a familiar story:
> I wasted money.
> I am a failure.
> Why can't I change this silly habit?
> What is wrong with me?

This short but powerful story brought up so much shame. Many stories I hold do. And in true Emily fashion, right before I would feel the full wave of discomfort of that shame, I would bury the thoughts away, thinking that if I stopped them in their tracks before they get the best of me that maybe it wouldn't ruin my day.

But all that burying isn't burying at all
It is an unfinished thought
A broken sentence
A noun waiting for the verb
Lingering in the air

And since I left it lingering
It transforms into guilt so heavy that as my lungs breathe it in
It moves through my blood into every organ
And it becomes a part of me

Imagine sitting in the same spot for too long and your leg falls asleep. As you stand up, it starts to wake up, sending the most bizarre and painful nerve signals through and through. But you don't cut it off. You let the pain happen despite all its annoyance because you need your leg back.

At some point you realize that you are your own limiting factor.

Maybe I could take something back by letting myself finally finish the sentence, despite all the discomfort.

For the first time, I opened the journals. I saw them not through a lens of judgement, but through a lens of curiosity. Sitting on these pages were the best of intentions with those Day 1 and Day 2 diary entries, but my writing was being done in a way that I thought you were supposed to write: with rules, with structure, with dates, with patterns.

I have always done things my way, yet here I was seeing myself attempt and fail, start and stop, always assuming I was the problem - not the system.

What if I did things my way?
No system
No rules
and most of all...
No pressure.

I found a pack of a green fuzzy journals I liked on Amazon and two days later I started writing. No rules, no structure, no dates, no patterns. It worked like magic. The release that my body and soul had craved for years poured out of me, page after page after page. I had taken back a part of me that was shut off. I was breathing fresh air again.

After notebook after notebook filled up with squiggles, poems, to-do lists, and flow charts, I sat with them all. Seeing things go from A to Z, watching the journey of on-paper scribbles to my new reality.

Sometimes I would laugh and feel proud, but many moments I was taken aback about what I'd written, surprised at the weight these sentences held, lines that effortlessly poured out. I was reading my notebooks I myself had filled as if I had never read them at all.

And for the very first time,
I saw my darkness and my heaviness
that my heart can so easily carry
in a form that was
                beautiful.

These journals allowed me to fall in love with my own shadows
because now the shadows
       the hard
       the dark to the shine
finally had a name and a face
(and sometimes they would even rhyme).

I went through every notebook I had, marking every chapter that made me feel something. I compiled them together and put them into this book you are now holding.

We cannot truly love our light without first loving our darkness.
                Without the darkness, we are nothing.

This is my most vulnerable expression of "I AM HUMAN", just like you. There is no human without fear, doubt, insecurity, pain, heartbreak. There is also no human without resilience, power, magic and beauty.

I have divided this book into 4 parts:

>DO
>FEEL
>KNOW
>MAKE

The journey of one into the next
The story that I've been seeing
A side of me I want you to know
Human being to human being.

I am so happy you are here.

Em

One day, not that long ago, I was having a very bad day.
Everything sucked.
I sucked.
My job sucked.
I hated it all.

I climbed into my bathtub, turned off the lights, let it all go and cried.

I didn't just cry… I ugly sobbed. I don't always let myself have those moments so when I hear something in the sky say "BABY GIRL LET THAT SHIT GO", I listen.

And within that sobbing and weeping, I had a vision.

It was me, holding something heavy overhead: a long stick with a basket on each side. I had no idea where I was or what I was doing, but I looked like the Emily I strive to be every day: making things look easy, making the most out of life with effort, making chocolate cake out of lemons and leaving bitches wondering how I did it.

I looked STRONG.

But strong me started to change. Sweat started to come off my forehead. My muscles started to shake. My convincing face turned into an "oh-shit" face and I no longer looked so sturdy.

I held on
I held on
I held on

Until I couldn't hold on anymore.

I dropped it all.

The pole overhead, the baskets on each side
        crumbled all around me

And I wept
And wept
And wept

I felt like a failure, not just in a "let's all go home, we did our best" way, but in the kind of way that your soul breaks in half and you can't see straight.

And then when I finally opened my eyes

I realized that within the baskets, there were soil and seeds
And without my knowing,

my tears that could not stop flowing
had let those seeds
 grow
grow
GROW
 GROW

in that moment I realized

it is not my strength that the world needs to know

It is my pain
It is my sadness
It is my heart on my sleeve
From the notebooks that I carry,
   the sentences that I weave

it is the funny thoughts in my head
that are usually right before bed

the dips and the valleys that come in front of the highs
the lightbulbs and the YES's and the "Oh shit that's WHY"s

I'm not a storyteller or a poet
I am simply someone who FEELS IT ALL

And that is how this book began.

Welcome to my process.

DO

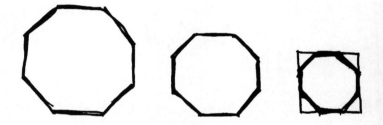

I was an octagon trying to be a square

Wishing away my angles
My surface area simply an inconvenience
        Not a place to explore

Trying every way to feel a little less
The extra square inches feeling too heavy
        No one else must feel this

Finding every reason to avoid those tiny angles
Dark and complicated with too much to say
        Better off we ignore

And since an octagon can't mold into a square

I shrunk.

> when we are scared shitless
> ↓
> we still decide it's better to jump
> ↓
> the jump teaches you more about your soul than any book, poem, podcast, guru could ever teach you

I AM NOT IMPERVIOUS TO fear or doubt. My mom had to pay me $2 to start soccer when I was four. I took 20 minutes to jump off my first diving board. It took me 25 years to not shake while speaking in front of crowds bigger than 15 people.

I've doubted every square inch of my soul and body: what all those inches were here for, if they were right, why they were

DO

different, and what made them qualified to hold the lines that I held.

At some point the doubting gets old.

It eats away at you with every conversation you have.
It becomes a part of you with every mirror that you walk by.
It follows you to dressing rooms
        to dinner dates
                to the next big interview that might change your life.

DO

It is ALL CONSUMING and you realize you've spent
so much time gnawing at your angles to be a square in a
WORLD OF SQUARES that you don't even know
who you are anymore.

DOUBT

The antidote to doubt is to DO.

Do more that makes you trust yourself.
Do more that makes you realize the things that feel big really aren't that big.
Do something you've doubted,
    again and again and again.
And when you no longer doubt it, find something new.
Tell yourself that you cannot, should not, and will not live in doubt.
We must DO, DO, DO.

> Tell yourself that you cannot, should not and will not live in doubt.
> Tell yourself that you cannot, should not and will not live in doubt.
> Tell yourself that you cannot, should not and will not live in doubt.
> Tell yourself that you cannot, should not and will not live in doubt.
> Tell yourself that you cannot, should not and will not live in doubt.

You have two options:

Option 1:

Will I continue to mold who I am and be uncomfortable (trying to be a square when I am so not a square)

or

Option 2:

Will I try something new simply knowing that I will be uncomfortable (because it is uncomfortable for everyone.)

It is really all quite uncomfortable, but only one discomfort will reap a reward.

- What was something you did that you are proud of?
- What was the last thing you tried that you were nervous about?
- When was the last time you did something slightly terrifying (and survived)?
- When's the last time you pushed yourself to get to know all those angles we are told to avoid?

If you haven't felt blissful in a while, I guarantee the reason is directly connected with the four questions above. If the answer doesn't come easy or you start to realize it's been a while since you've felt BLISS, we can start right here.

Update the answer on one of those four questions. Maybe even do it today.

List of things I'd like to ~~try~~ Do

-
-
-
-

DO

Trying is the PLAN B, or C or D or E
        those not-so-distant shores that you can always see
Trying says we will still get wet without fully jumping in
        And if it disappoints you, you didn't really expect to win
Trying gives us permission when we don't get the results we crave
        To point the finger and pivot, instead of just being brave
Because TRYING is the safe zone, it takes the pain out of the fall
        & we exchange the bumps & bruises for choosing to stay small

DO

Trying means you have options…
And options don't require you to grow

                                        demand growth.

DO

During my first saxophone solo I was so nervous that my mouth dried up and when it finally was my long-anticipated turn I started to blow air and instead of the sound I expected to hear it squeaked so loud that it hurt everyone's ears

And I faked playing the rest of the concert

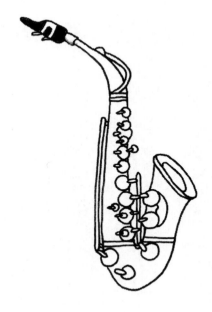

DO

Sometimes you don't want to DO because you don't think
you'll do a good enough job
You'll let someone down
Or you'll let yourself down

And so you sit
        and
        rot.

DO

We assume: people are naturals
We assume that luck had the biggest part to play
We assume or they might be different because they make it look easy

    We forget everyone's voice was once shaky
    We forget that fear doesn't care who you are
    We forget and it requires facing your worst, take after take

        We forget
        because no one is brave enough to talk about it

dear legs

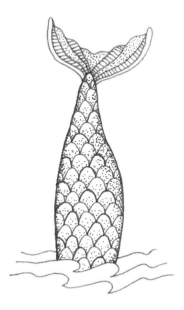

I need to apologize
for the things
    I thought about you
    said about you
    wished away about you
you tried to teach me things I wasn't willing to hear
bounded in my thoughts, captured by my fear
as if something about me just didn't add up
or I added up too much, too much for one cup

i spent so many hours fighting you
every single piece that looked back
the thoughts I wouldn't dare tell anyone
and the deleted photographs

all on things the world couldn't even see

DO

    too wrapped up to just simply BE
        lies we tell ourselves
        that become the foundation of our fate
    the fate that was handed off to broken people
        and without their permission, we sit and wait?

as if the sound of my heart isn't the sound of the world
    moving

or

everything I love
everything I smile at
everything I marvel at
everything I can not get enough of

    is just another version of me

this is long overdue
the idea of finally falling in love with YOU
    the old man laugh
    the lines that it makes
    the crease in your eyebrows
    how your hair wakes

        up
        up
        up

the time we spend on wishing away our body
    the time is
        UP

preventing us from living
    expanding
    breathing

being as big as the mountain
BECAUSE YOU ARE THE MOUNTAIN

shrug
    and there will be landslides
the world will crack
if you choose to

take it back
take it back
take it back

you are not the painter
or the paint

                you are what is on the canvas

DO

~~List of things I wish I would have done but didn't because I was so afraid of how much the fall would have hurt~~
List of things I almost didn't do because I didn't give myself time to think about how much it would hurt and/or someone convinced me that it was worth the risk:
- Start soccer when I was 4
- Jump off a diving board
- Speak to more than 15 people in a group
- Start my own business
- Start four more
- Start a podcast
- Write this book

The more you think, the less you do.

DO

When doing **is** enough:

The doing gives you guts.
The doing gives you belief in yourself.
The doing is your guiding light.
The doing is euphoric.
The doing is **addictive**.

CRUISE CONTROL: THE POINT AT which you know you can get away with driving at the speed you are currently driving at without the fear of getting pulled over. It allows you to take your foot off the gas pedal; it gives you permission to sit back and stay comfy, even if just for a bit.

Unlike the common conversation of "DO THINGS THAT MAKE YOU UNCOMFORTABLE", I have a tendency to be afraid of COMFORT.

If you've ever believed something, truly believed it, and it turned out to be untrue… It changes you.

DO

I didn't want to get hurt
I didn't want to care too much
I didn't want to be disappointed
I didn't want to be fooled*

So I always did the uncomfortable thing: the DOING. Foot on the gas. There were no options BUT that. If I sat still too long, if I knew the result, if I became familiar with the comfort… then it could bite again.

drop out of college
reality is
move to colorado
compete in everything
start my own business
compete in more things
launch a Kickstarter
speak in front of strangers
put myself out there
do things that terrify me

Whether it was jumping out of airplanes
Riding my motorcycle a little too fast
Competing in things as often as possible
Launching another business

It was always "what's next what's next what's next", checking off boxes on an imaginary list, rarely feeling pride and always feeling late to the party. How could I be proud? I was still so far from where I needed to go.

I refused cruise control.

I pressed hard and although my body wanted to slow down, I ignored it. I ignored it until my ability to do what was next on my list became harder and harder to do. My "DOING", which

---

* And maybe even a little bit deeper
I didn't want myself to be happy
   Because happy means you might find out it's all a lie again

was my identity, was now being compromised. That is when I finally started to listen.

I realized maybe I cared too much about too little of things.

And then I thought about it some more…

If I couldn't be my dream weight, why get on the scale and weigh?
If I couldn't play soccer at my dream college, why would I even play?
If I couldn't do Crossfit without always improving, why keep all the pressure on my head?
If I couldn't be all of it all of the time, then I might as well be dead.

I completely quit caring about the things that I couldn't care completely about.

DO

**What is the middle
between giving all the shits
and giving none of the shits?**

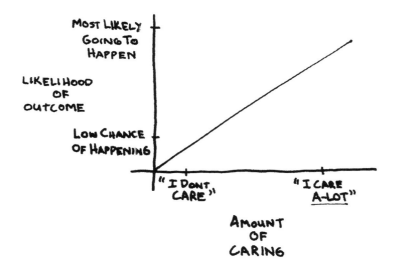

Maybe it's as simple as
we stop ourselves from caring too much
when we are unsure of the outcome

DO

I HAVE ALWAYS WONDERED WHETHER we have a "CARE CAPACITY". That we each are only allowed so much room to care about certain things, and we don't have a choice in the matter.

In other words: We each care **exactly** the same amount in total, but all at different percentages with all different things.

For example:

ME vs. GRIFF

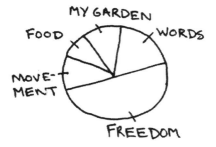

DO

No one wants to get a fruit bowl with just cantaloupe.

STEP ONE: QUALITY

WHEN WE ARE TRULY HONEST with ourselves (no ego, no fear, no judgement) we can start to think about the things we care about without a filter.

We only have one pie chart (or fruit bowl) to fill up. It is up to us to make sure it is filled with the things we actually want it to be filled up with.

When we realize how much CARING is done on the categories that we know are cantaloupe
(nothing special, not a lot of flavor, usually too crunchy and always out of season.)

DO

We start to get a little smarter about what we put our time into when it comes to caring. They all fill the same space.

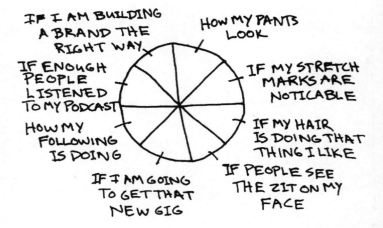

Honesty with how we think about ourselves allows us to change priorities fairly quickly to get the most out of that pie chart.

STEP TWO: VARIETY

Slowly but surely, we all learn to let go of the things that don't matter as much. We realize how much space they fill, and one by one, we can replace them.

As I replaced my insecurities with things I loved, i.e. "MY PASSIONS", I still found it hard to not be all-consumed by just a couple things.
If I stopped putting all my attention into those passions, I would feel immense guilt. I would still be eating that pineapple like I would die if I chose a melon.

> I cared too much about too little of things.

DO

And back to this all-too-real-for-me line of:
What is the middle between giving all the shits and giving none of the shits?

As much as I wish I could be like this:

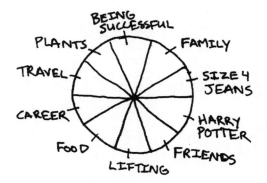

I tend to be more like this:

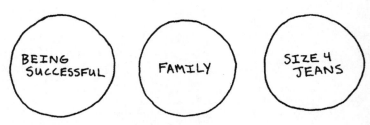

(I'm not really a natural at balance.)

I know this about myself just by looking at my track record. I used to be

THIS:

Then:

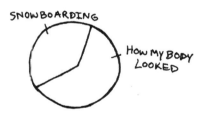

Then:

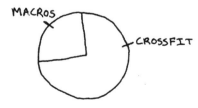

And I can tell you, my world was small.

DO

Both the bowl of cantaloupe and the bowl of pineapple were leaving me with the same result:

bored
unsettled
unsure
moody
tired
looking around wondering what the hell I was doing wrong when for a while it felt so right

Enter: CRUISE CONTROL.

The cruise control happens when it's time for something else in our Care Capacity Pie Chart to get a little gas. Where it first might feel that we are beginning to slack as we hit that cruise button might just be a sign that another category is joining the party.

And when more join the party, that is the:
    blackberries
    or raspberries
    or mangos
    or juicy delicious grapes
that we all wish we could get in a fruit bowl

In a world full of cantaloupe, be the fruit bowl that has the pineapple AND the raspberries AND the grapes.

DO

What's in your pie chart?

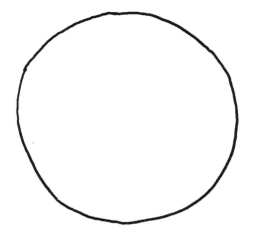

Add some new fruit.

(And get rid of the cantaloupe.)

DO

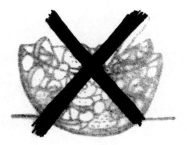

"it's a 'fuck the fruitbowl' kind of day"

On Resistance…

Resistance looks like the gloom on the cloud resting over your shadow
    the snappiness of your mood
    the skipped events that you booked
Resistance feels like the crash after the high
    The heaviness on your chest
    the pressure in your throat
Resistance sounds like silent sniffles in the shower
    The comments under your breathe
    The words "I JUST WANT TO BE HAPPY"
    When deep down you know why you aren't
We are masochists in our misery
And we want to take the whole ship down with us

DO

Resistance is quite simply the ICK that we feel that we know we can move out of, but we either

A: choose not to feel it or
B: choose to not do anything.

```
CHOOSE NOT              CHOOSE TO
TO FEEL IT              NOT DO
   ↓                       ANYthING
TYPE A                     ↓
RESISTANCE              TYPE B
                        RESISTANCE
```

Check all the boxes that apply.

You might be prone to TYPE A resistance if:

- ☐ You live a very busy life and like it that way (though sometimes complain about it being so busy)
- ☐ Sitting/being still feels like death (meditation is HARD)
- ☐ You are highly active, physically and/or mentally
- ☐ You love adrenaline rushes or are an adrenaline junkie
- ☐ You are obsessed with your fitness classes, usually more for the workout than for the people
- ☐ There is never a dull moment in your life because you don't let dull happen

DO

I WENT TO BAINBRIDGE AFTER the word caught my ear so strongly on a podcast I hosted* that I couldn't stop thinking about it. I soon was in Seattle, then on a ferry, then in a perfect cottage right by the sea.

It was gloomy, magical, Victorian, cozy. All the feelings that come when you know you are in exactly the right place at exactly the right time although you have no concept of how it lined up so perfectly. It just IS.

There were a few kayaks by the water. After a day, despite all the magic, I was getting a little restless. I grabbed a kayak and dragged it to the end of land, pushing it into the beginning of sea.

---

* Meathead Hippie® episode 93

DO

At that very moment, the wind blew so hard the kayak slammed back into me.
I tried again.
The wind blew again so hard that the piercing cold water sprayed on my body.
I tried again.
One foot in the water about to climb in the kayak, mission almost accomplished, and it started raining.
I stopped. I looked up at the dark sky. And as if it was some sort of epiphany of my soul finally connecting to my brain, I realized:

I really don't want to be wet.
I really don't want to be cold.

>But this is what I do
>But life happens on the other side of work
>But bliss happens on the other side of terror

But...
Sometimes easier is okay, too.
I pulled the kayak out of the sea, right onto land, and I sat in it.
No drama, no noise, no story.
Just a simple experience of me, simply conquering my fear of missing out on everything.

And the moment I sat down
The clouds above me parted
the sun shined down so brightly on me and my little kayak sitting on land
the rays of beautiful light hitting me, warming me, kissing my body
finding a type of joy in this complete surrender
that I never had known
that I have never been taught
that I have never experienced
>by taking an easier way

DO

I looked up again at the sky
and it spoke louder than I had ever heard:

                "It is about damn time."

TYPE A RESISTANCE ⟶ WHEN YOU ARE ADDICTED TO THE RESISTANCE

THE LEGS OF THIS RESISTANCE gained traction because I believed that in order to receive fulfillment of any nature, there must first and foremost be effort.

EFFORT = REWARD

Whether we came into the world believing this or we were trained to believe this, this is the natural cycle of receiving something we want.

DO

> I want to be healthier, I will eat more veggies and feel healthier.[*] (TRUE)
> I want to be better at __, therefore I will practice and be better. (TRUE)
> I want to heal my knee pain, I will take collagen and turmeric and heal faster. (TRUE)
> I want a different position at my job, therefore I will work hard and expand my skillset to earn it. (TRUE)
> I want a stronger body, therefore I will lift weights. (TRUE)

There is nothing wrong with this cycle of resistance and improvement, but what happens when we start to think that there is nothing GOOD that comes out of anything without effort? That in order to receive something, we must DO something.
In order to feel:
bliss
happiness
peace
JOY
one must make an effort, no matter what.
I must be ON the kayak in the turbulent water getting cold and wet in order to receive any sort of positive experience.

With that train of thought, let's try some more things we want:

- I want to be less stressed, I will do … less things?
- I want to feel less crazy, I will … sit still and meditate?
- In order to feel joy, we must… stop and look around?

LACK OF EFFORT ALSO CAN = REWARD

---

[*] #vegoutwithem

I lived my whole life seeing results from effort and hard work, so to teach my body to slow down and do less felt like I was cutting my legs off moments before climbing another mountain.

By dissecting the long-winding road of my brain and my habits, I have come to the conclusion that this nagging feeling of being unsettled came from the belief that if I wasn't DOING something I was missing out on everything.

> Contentment = FOMO
> Contentment = I won't be ready
> Contentment = complacency
> Contentment = terrifying

No matter how many times I spun this around in my head, knowing that it was illogical and ridiculous or that I should just allow my mind to relax, I couldn't. There was just no amount of self-talk, podcasts, books, mezcal, or marijuana that allowed me to feel that way. If I wasn't busy or moving or DOING, I could not be content because I was too busy feeling there was so much left to do.

If doing a lot of doing got us everywhere, there wouldn't be a problem with the way I was operating. I would be writing a book on how to DO DO DO because I am really fucking good at the word DO. But it wasn't getting me everywhere. After a while it stopped getting me anywhere at all. I was spinning and spinning in circles, desperate for answers in more doing because that's the only thing I knew.

The thing is, reward cannot come from JUST effort because it shuts off our ability to receive.

DO

We stay on one side of this cycle yet wonder why we are
tired
resentful
exhausted
sad

And we are tired, resentful, exhausted, and sad because in order to keep this beautiful cycle balanced and to find a little peace in that space between your ears... you must receive.

DO

This surrender is always easier said than done, so if you are like me and maybe have a tendency to have TYPE A resistance, maybe this can help:

Check the boxes of all that apply:

- ☐ I am a good human
- ☐ I do things at work that help the world in some way
- ☐ I do things outside of work that help the world in some way
- ☐ I compliment people
- ☐ I open the door for strangers
- ☐ I tip well
- ☐ I show my love to the people I love through words, gifts, acts of service, time, touch (and asking questions)
- ☐ I look people in the eye when they talk to me
- ☐ I listen to people

YOU ALWAYS DO.

It is time to RECEIVE.

THE SECOND TYPE OF RESISTANCE can best be described as this:

I have a problem (I don't feel joy).
I know exactly what I could do to fix said problem.
I do everything BUT the thing that will help, and/or I do nothing.

I then hate myself the whole time because I know what I could do to help
Yet I am being a total masochist
And now I feel GUILT and SHAME on top of the problem

And this just sucks.

DO

I have struggled with both types of resistance but TYPE B holds more shadows than TYPE A. There is an option that you could CHOOSE to do (that would fix it all) hanging right in front of you:

> Laugh at the joke. Go work out. Make the salad. Turn off the TV and read the book. Get off Instagram and call your mom. Paint a little.* Write a little. Go outside. Say no to the third cookie. Take the supplements. Go to the new gym that just opened. Snuggle. Try the dance class. Invite your friend over for dinner. Get on the motorcycle. Take the rest of the day off.

But we don't do it.

we are frozen green
            failures
             frauds
             POSs
             shitty people.

So if "JUST CHOOSE JOY" isn't working out for you that well either...

Where do we go?

To the bees.

---

* I love you, Judy.

A series of haikus:

we seek out our joy
and we effort happiness
struggling to find

buzzing all around
feeling in the wrong places
all at the wrong time

a little too late
so much work with no return
and we stop trying

so are you the bee?
Or can we be the flower
Finally not flying

The act of being
Simply attracting your joy
As it comes to you

as your petals glow
what you seek will find you too.[*]
(you are not the bee)

---

[*] "what you seek is seeking you." –rumi

DO

It never worked for me to see joy as a choice. Whether it was my rebel mentality or my stubbornness in those days I needed joy the most, to understand that my job is not to DO but to simply BE

Be who I am (the flower)
With the light that I have (even when dim)
Unapologetic
Unhiding
Unashamed
THIS IS WHO I AM TODAY, PEOPLE
Only then would joy find me

Some days joy finds me easier
Because that light is a little brighter
        And I remember to love those days a little bit more each time

(on joy)

The days you forget who you are
Allow you to love even more the days you find yourself again

DO

Your
light
is
always
brighter
when
you're
not
worried
about
how
bright
it
is.

I feel calm (I don't usually feel calm)
I have no preferences (I always have preferences)
I could be neither here nor there (I'm always here or there)

Is something wrong with me?

I think I am letting my edge go away
      my edge is what makes me great
           my edge is why I am even here

CONTENTMENT IS TERRIFYING

DO

Always ready for battle.

DO

How can you expect to experience joy with so much to prove?

The only war is the one in your own head.

DO

The resistance I forgot to mention:

the thoughts in our own heads not allowing us to be still in our body
To acknowledge that all is well
And be at peace
No "I should" to be had
With no "need to" to do
No box to check
And nothing to scroll
just be content

Which means that I might not be ready for whatever is right around the corner
        for the battle that I have to win
        for the fight that I have to fight
        for the hurt that I must shield myself from
 With my armor that is
                so
              damn
              heavy
 But without it I am weak
              (and exposed)

Who is going to be the one to finally tell me
That the war is over
                …and it has been for years.

DO

I don't know how to put down the armor.

DO

progress is looking up from looking down
without a kink in your neck
because you start catching yourself soon enough
and although it's still bad you avoid the pain from reactive
as we learn to fall in love with the word prevent
and although it feels so far because
"Straighten up!" is still screaming in your head from your
mom or dad or teacher
(and maybe it will never leave you)
You still noticed it in time
And your neck thanks you

DO

Knowing you have armor that might not be needed anymore is sometimes all it takes.

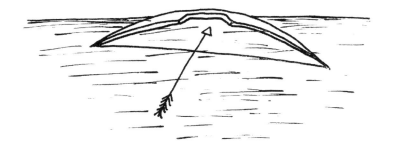

DO

my tendency to see the bad before the good
                    is a defense mechanism

There is a place where peace must live
Rooftops the same
Lawns watered
2-car garages if lucky
Cookie-cutter homes
That must be peace
A phantom of one's wishes
An idea
That becomes the standard
Which all began to chase

And since it doesn't exist
We judge harshly our
Heat
We judge harshly our
Cold
                        And figure out that lukewarm is safe

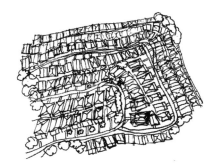

DO

Impatience is the ultimate sign of immaturity.*

---

* things gardening has taught me

DO

We beg for it - pray for it - wish for it
When it's right in front of you
Will you even notice?

DO

I have too many books
And too little of seconds
I move too quickly
And yet never fast enough
My heart is overflowing
Sometimes so quickly that it empties
And I am left with a shoulder shrug
And a gentle pat on the back
That it was bound to happen
At some point.

And when it's about to sputter out completely
The universe reminds me
Why I am here
Why I exist
And how the beauty in giving that dollar to the man on the corner
And being tagged in someone's transformation
And someone giving me a hug over a hot cup of tea

All becomes like the jazz playing in my ear

beautiful chaos…

Refill
Reboot
Refocus

You are needed

FEEL

FEEL

I got really good at DOING because I was avoiding so much FEELING.

I would love for you to help me with my theory that the majority of us could be divided into two categories:

Those who are really good at DOING, but tend to avoid the FEELING

                        #iamadoer

&

Those that are really good at FEELING, but tend to have a hard time with the DOING

                        #iamafeeler

FEEL

It took me a very long time to learn that I was using DOING as a way to not be FEELING, and it was a mix of muggles and wands that taught me it.

The first time I ever questioned the way I was being raised
Was when the pastor preached about Harry Potter being the devil
I was intrigued
And I naturally wanted to read
    something so forbidden
When we left and started it all from scratch
The Harry Potter books were my first books[*]
And now were all mine
Becoming the person in the line
    I devoured them
They represented freedom, imagination
a new possibility
A life only I could think up
Starting with what my creativity could see

---

[*] thank you, Aunt Sue

As soon as I finished reading and watching all 7
I read them all again
Lightning bolt on my head
    Never wanting to go to bed
Not just about the magic
But the story of the writer
Rejected rejected rejected
    She believed in something
And now I did too

A few years later I realized I hadn't seen them in so long
A marathon on TV inspired a week of Harry Potter
My favorite series in the world
Ready to reminisce and remember

But as I watched
I realized I didn't remember anything
It was all a giant blur
Details not even coming back after they happen
Watching it like it was the first time

I spent the first part of the week arguing with myself
Crease in my forehead
Thinking it would all come back
And maybe I would remember the important stuff
But it never did

My whole life was about doing
Doing
Doing
Even when I'm watching something so important to me
I'm doing
Thinking
multi-tasking
elsewhere

FEEL

Not in my body
Not in the present

It wasn't about Harry Potter
It was about the realization of the years I ran away from
anything that made me still
And in the front of my mind piled and piled
all the moments I had missed because of it

The conversations
The friendships
The delicate details

And I finally noticed for the first time
what felt like an elephant sitting on my head
       all this doing
         finally caught up

FEEL

The light at the end of the tunnel in 12 steps:

Step 1: seeing the light at the end of the tunnel
Step 2: working towards the light at the end of the tunnel
Step 3: working towards the light at the end of the tunnel
Step 4: working towards the light at the end of the tunnel
Step 5: working towards the light at the end of the tunnel
Step 6: working towards the light at the end of the tunnel
Step 7: working towards the light at the end of the tunnel
Step 8: realizing the light isn't getting any closer
Step 9: trying new ways to get the light closer
Step 10: realizing the light STILL isn't getting any closer
Step 11: complete depression
Step 12: finally understanding there is no light at the end of the tunnel

The light allowed you to begin.

FEEL

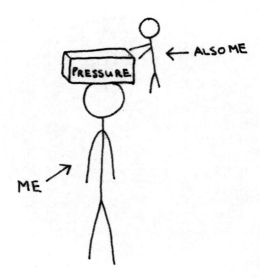

Scattered
AF
Just unsure of even where to begin

All the pressure
First pressure from me
But now because
I don't just stop

FEEL

You are small
And cracked like the desert from a million miles high
Dreaming of being quenched
By the very thing staring back at you

The face-off of all:
To see what you can be
But neither touch, nor try, nor be close enough
That it becomes reality

It flies by
A glimpse of what could be
What should be
What isn't but what
IS IS IS

Because it IS you
Too soon too far too gone
For now

FEEL

the chip on my shoulder
the dark shadow that's looking back
I judge
  kick
  scream
  at the very thing that is
  myself.

FEEL

Today I am tired
My own voice yelling at myself
To keep grinding
To keep moving
To just pick it up

Those moments are the most powerful
The balance between what sets you apart
and what will break you

It will take years to perfect
The art of listening to your body
Hear what it is saying
Respect it
Honor it
And understand that some days
You'll pick up that stone
And some days you'll tell that
stone
"I will see you tomorrow"

How do we know when we've done too much doing and not enough feeling?

We are tired
        we are tired
                we are tired

To feel things means to **not run away from them**.

So we sit and we feel and we hate it.

I grew up on Nancy Drew, Matlock, and John Grisham. I still want to be a spy and if I ever have the chance to, I think I would make a great one.

My solution to anything I hate is simply this…

GET CURIOUS.
        Curiosity saved my life

I hated my acne. I got curious about my acne. I fixed my acne.
I hated my stomach pains. I got curious about my stomach pains. I fixed my stomach pains.
I hated my job. I got curious about a new job. I fixed my job.

I hated sitting and feeling and not doing. I got curious about my resistance to feeling. I got better at sitting and feeling and not doing.

I believe you can easily find the resistance in your body when you are curious enough about it, the problem is we are too busy doing that we haven't given ourselves the chance.

Is it in your throat because you have so much to say but no ears to say it to?
Is it in your gut because something just doesn't feel right?
Is it heavy on your heart
Or an elephant sitting on your head?

And then we ask…

WHY WHY WHY

what was the conversation . what was the comment . what is the thing you wish you could have said . what is the to list . what is the thing you are avoiding . what is the thing that you are pushing down down down that is coming up up up .

Put down the armor and stop buzzing like a bee.
Start asking WHY so you can finally be free.

FEEL

you will never get used to a dripping sink

you can convince yourself it's not that bad

but it's always there

drip

consuming you

drip

driving you insane

drip

in the back of your mind as if that part of your mind is some vacant storage unit, unimportant

drip

but it's still your mind

drip

already expended

drip

already worn-out

drip

this is what it's like to be busy, it's normal

drip

we can fix it next week

drip

FEEL

PROBLEM PATHWAY:

- sit with it
  - ↓
  - move through it

- avoidance
  - ↓
  - push it down
  - ↓
  - get better at avoiding
  - ↓
  - let it bubble up in another form.

You are **not** your thoughts.
You are **not** your thoughts.
You are **not** your thoughts.
You are **not** your thoughts.
You are **not** your thoughts.
You are **not** your thoughts.
You are **not** your thoughts.

>Just like I was not my bad skin
>Just like I was not my stomach pains
>Just like I was not the job I fucking hated
>>**you** are not your thoughts.

Feeling something is not to **be** something.
It makes it easier to be **more** inquisitive
when a feeling is separate from **you.**

you > your thoughts

and when we cannot pinpoint a feeling
or we ask and the answer doesn't come
we remember sometimes there is no reason at all for a feeling…
       it just IS.

even if it's inside our brains
       it is not our brain
           and it'll go away when it's ready to

FEEL

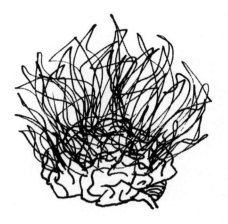

I think the world's biggest travesty is the "art of doing things at half capacity"

If you are going to feel
Feel IT COMPLETELY

>	Let it consume you
>	Let it rip you in half
>	Let it swallow you whole
>	Let it burn you alive
>	Let it drown you

And when you finally catch your breathe
                & see the light

There will be no coming back to the other side

FEEL

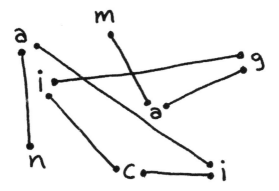

Because crazy is where the magic happens.

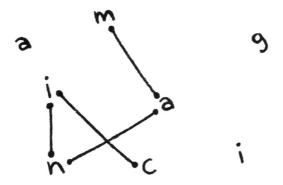

We all are told to be grateful
"3 things of gratitude every morning
will turn your day around"
But when your head won't talk to your heart?
It simply feels like a load of shit.

The days I needed to remind myself the most of what I
    had
And how far I had come
The words were empty
Because there was too far to go

Gratitude starts deep within your soul
And by the time it moves from your cells to your spine
    up to your brain
It is not just a list on a piece of paper

FEEL

It is the tap of the hand
        on the steering wheel to the beat
The humming in your throat
        As your breath and voice meet

It is the grin that turns into a smile
        As you let something funny fill your face
And on the best of days it turns to laughter
        As you allow yourself to fill some space

It is the way the trees move
        when the wind starts to speak
and the taste of red wine
        when you finish a hard week

it is your herbs in the garden growing
        the weather that is just right
the perfect call with your sister
        and your white shirt staying white

    It is all around
    And it is neither an action nor a verb
    It in fact is lack of action
    it is simply BEING
    and seeing
    and finally
    finally
    finally

    FEELING.

GRATEFUL FOR:

- Griff
- my garden
- my espresso machine
- the people who love me
- my house
- my brain
- my nail color
- my fireplace
- my body
- mezcal

FEEL

I went on a run today and I didn't need music.*

---

* ways I know I'm getting better at feeling

Gratitude digs up the layers.

FEEL

The demons you fight:

7. I am unsure of the purpose of any of this. I feel isolated, I feel alone.
6. I am stuck in white space and in my own thoughts. I am repeating the same story.
5. I can't figure out what to say or how to even say it. I am ashamed of what I wish for.
4. I can't forgive. I am resentful. I have so many walls.
3. I have so much guilt and shame. I feel undeserving.
2. I feel out of control. I am moody. I feel powerless in my environment.
1. I have no confidence in myself or my abilities. I hate who I am. I feel empty.

The ways to fight them:

7. My limitations are always self-imposed. When I realize I am a channel for all ideas, and the universe is conspiring to help me succeed, I will become limitless.
6. When I feel limited it is because I need to work on myself, and by working on myself I will recreate my story.
5. My voice means nothing without purpose and I choose to use my voice with that purpose.
4. I have love like the oceans, and I choose to lead with my heart not my brain.
3. I am a creative genius and a channel for anything that needs to be said. My creativity is my abundance.
2. I am a powerful being. Anything I desire starts right within me.
1. I am safe in my body. I am safe right here, right now. I am at home because I am my own home.

FEEL

IN ORDER TO FEEL MORE, we need to clean up the DOs. We clean it up by getting the "I should be doing this…"s out of your life.

FEEL

Immediately upon finishing a
> Task
> Workout
> Meeting
> Conversation
> Interview
> Coffee date
> Normal date
> Book
> Netflix episode
> Phone call

Ask yourself

"Do I feel energized?
OR
"Do I feel drained?

My DO brain was on auto-pilot and I realized as I got better at my FEEL brain, I was making my life a whole lot harder than it needed to be.

FEEL

These 10 things make me feel ENERGIZED

1.

2.

3.

4.

5.

6.

7.

8.

9.

10.

FEEL

These 10 things make me feel DRAINED

1.

2.

3.

4.

5.

6.

7.

8.

9.

10.

Your right to feel energized > your "duty" of doing draining things.

Doing the things that drain you = doing the things you <u>think you SHOULD</u> be doing

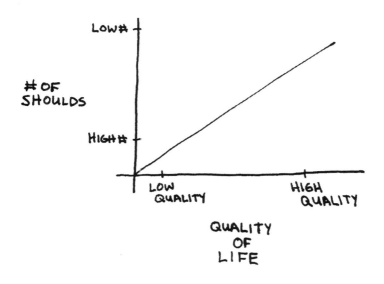

FEEL

You know what else we don't like sitting in?
COMPLIMENTS.

COMPLIMENTS 1-0-1:[*]

"those jeans look good on you"
~~"I got them on sale"~~
~~"oh really thanks they are old"~~
~~"they feel a little tight"~~
~~"I feel like a fat pig but thank you!"~~
"I feel pretty good in them myself, thank you."
                    (You, this week. Try it.)

---
[*] receiving 1-0-1

FEEL

It comes in waves
And before it crashes
It feels like it's been gone forever
  You think it's never coming back
That it's over
And not worth it anymore

Then the crash
Hits so hard
Your breath is gone
And you realize again
That it is just like

poetry
Or art
Or music
Or A life boat

When it's there you can't imagine where you would be
    without it

FEEL

you don't
notice the
clouds move
until you
stop and watch
them

KNOW

KNOW

---
* the art of manifestation

And the final piece, the art of KNOWING

If this triangle could talk, it would simply say:
You must DO to move through doubt
You must FEEL, both the good and the bad and
You must KNOW you are worth it

And that is how things happen.

It does not say:
You must DO to move through doubt
You must FEEL, both the good and the bad
You must **start to think** that you are worth it
or you must **kind of think** that you are worth it
or you are **going to stare in the mirror and try to convince your brain** that you are worth it

This final piece involves
re-training every cell in your being
re-routing every thought in your mind
re-writing every story you have ever told
re-re-re-re-re-re-re repeat

UNTIL
YOU
KNOW
YOU
ARE
WORTH
IT.

KNOW

    I wish to feel as brave
         as I appear
    as unstoppable as a current
    no longer in moments or bursts
         (which makes me think it was just chance)

    but to walk in it
    breathe in it
    LIVE IN IT

KNOW

The things that make your eyes roll
while you are scrolling on your phone
The times you loathed every second
but 3-2-1 ACTION and a smile is shown

The fights with your person
that spin round and round and round
The wounds that feel salted
because the WHY we still haven't found

We mostly know these demons
The ones we never admit we keep
We hold them as our safety net
Because we fear going in too deep

KNOW

WE HAVE HEARD MANY A time that the people in our life who bother us the most are simply mirroring back the things we haven't solved in ourselves: jealousy. anger. frustration. annoyance.

But here's the beautiful reality that no one talks about: mirroring ourselves cannot go one way without it also being the other. **The people in our life that we ADMIRE are also mirroring back the things that we hold inside.**

Think about some **things** you are:
obsessed with
can't get enough of
make your heart want to EXPLODE

Or think about the **humans** you are:
obsessed with
can't get enough of
make your heart want to EXPLODE

And start to wrap your mind around the fact that you admire them so much because you too embody those qualities.

Since it taken me approximately 30 years to admit the level if my own personal self-loathing, let me show you how I got to this conclusion by way of the person this book is dedicated to, the one who teaches me unconditional love on the daily, and the one who screams "YOU ARE MY CHAMPION" when she drops me off at the airport…

My mom.

First write down:
WHO YOU ADMIRE THE MOST AND WHAT TRAITS
you love about that person
(don't look ahead)

Person you admire	why

My mom's answers:

Person I admire	why
Mother Teresa	she saw every human being as worthy of love.
Eleanor Roosevelt	she deeply cared about human rights. she did things she was scard to do = brave

KNOW

I wish you all could meet my mom.
She sees every human for who they are, and loves them unconditionally. She also is the bravest human I have ever met.
My mom IS Mother Theresa and Eleanor Roosevelt mixed in with full-moon ceremonies.
Those who she admires have always been those who she embodies.

Those we admire bring out our best
    because it exists inside us
While those we hate bring out our worst
    because that also can exist inside us

write down:
WHO YOU ADMIRE THE MOST AND WHAT TRAITS you have in COMMON

Person you admire	traits you have in common

KNOW

SEE THE WORST
Release all judgement for it
Thank it for speeding up your growth

Repeat about 888x
And eventually, it gets smaller
                        And smaller
                        And smaller
                        And smaller
                        And smaller
                        And smaller
                        And smaller
                        And smaller
                        And smaller
                        And smaller

SEE THE BEST
Release the belief that celebrating your best is
egotistical/self-centered/self-absorbed/unnecessary
Thank it for speeding up your growth

Repeat about 888x
And eventually, it gets
                And bigger
                And bigger
                And bigger
                And bigger
                And bigger
                And bigger
                And bigger
                And bigger
                And bigger

KNOW

>
> There are moments, people, events that inspire you
> How would I do up there
> What would I say if they asked me that
> I want to be that too

That is not a coincidence
That is a KNOWING

If you can think it
You can be it
If you can think it
you can be it

we are too busy thinking our way OUT of it
we have too few of the right people IN it

KNOW

Without the knowing:

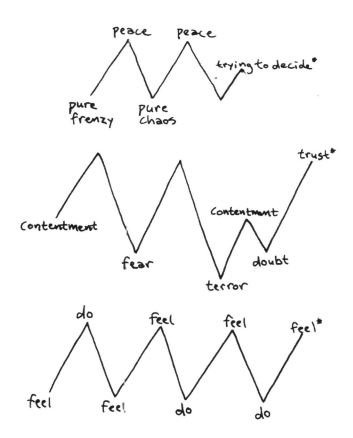

---
*when the KNOW is lacking

KNOW

The knowing is the hardest part
because it involves
trust.

You must trust that there is a peace in the stability
    Without needing the ups to feel alive

You must trust that you will keep overflowing
    Without fearing if it will survive

You must trust that you deserve to feel so much bliss
    without worrying everything will go to shit if
    you do

You must trust that you are on the exact right path
    without looking for more walls to push
    through

The knowing is the hardest part
because it involves
trust.

My heart
Holds oceans
Yet can crack like the desert

Maybe the chambers we learned about in school have it all wrong
Or are only half the story

There can be so much love flowing out
But it's still only half of your heart

When did we fall out of love with ourselves?

The topic of self-love can so easily be over-simplified to "look in the mirror and love who you are." Some days you feel like a Rockstar, and some days you feel like a paper sack. Nobody is going to love a paper sack, not even the paper sack. Let's stop over-simplifying it.

We all know we have walls, barriers, protection mechanisms, and traits that are purely NURTURE. Family stuff, sibling stuff, and growing-up stuff is not easy.

Then on top of that we have belief systems and hand-me-downs that we were just born with. Nurture AND Nature.

KNOW

Lucky us.

When we feel so much for others, it's hard to understand why we cannot feel that for ourselves, too. It feels impossible to look at yourself the same way you would look at someone you love, but until you do, the love you have for others is still only half of what you could give.

We look away from the mirror because it's ugly and uncomfortable: we never want to see the worst of ourselves.

We see split ends
We see blackheads
We see big thighs
We see fear
We see doubt
We see insecurity
We see anger

We see a person we don't want to be anymore, yet here we are looking straight at it. And staring at it brings up all the things no one ever wants to feel.

The guilt storm always ends up in "I AM THE WORST PERSON EVER". You know what that mentality brings you? The worst things. The worst people. The worst life.

We can do much, much better than the worst. That means we must start with the guilt we feel when we see parts of ourselves we don't like.

Guilt is not your guide nor is it your god.

When we get
 c u r i o u s
about the guilt, we can transform it from ominous and terrifying to something tangible.

Every part of you, the good AND the bad, exists to serve you in some way.

KNOW

I wonder if oysters know what manifests inside their walls
Without that hard, bumpy outer shell
(that doesn't look so pretty at first)
There would be no way for an oyster to survive
        Years of the ocean
        Turbulent waves
        Hungry sea creatures
There would be no home for the magic that occurs when somehow a parasite
SNEAKS it's way in
Triggering layer after layer of protection
The process [*]
Of harmful to beautiful
Innate intelligence, simply protecting itself
Creating the most beautiful transformation

        I also wonder how many pearls are never found.

---

[*] another gift of the sea, dedicated to Vanilla Bean

KNOW

The layers of sand between that big beautiful ocean and the rim
 of your heart
might be thin or might be the Sahara
but that desert didn't make itself up.
It allowed you to have any ocean at all.

No matter how much ocean you hold, and no matter how much
 desert you have
 we must remember it was at some point our way to protect
 who we were.

 refuse to let the lines blur:
 who we were.
 who we were.
 who we were.

 Not who we are. Not who we wish to be.

KNOW

White, with green, & smells of pine
You feel so lost until messages, pokes, a breeze of hope hits you
And you don't feel so far from what you've always wanted

We are all just holding our breath
Checking the mirror too many times
Dreaming while awake, singing a song through desperate exhales
A tune that was never meant to be ours

And as it slips
We defy gravity by holding
Gripping so tightly
Our only focus is to not let go
Don't let go
Keep it
Even though it was never meant to be ours

And when the smell of pine fills our breath
Or the breeze melts it all away

You remember again who you are
And the LET GO
Begins

THE LET GO.

Catch and release: except we tend to just catch.

KNOW

Write 3 things you do not like about yourself.

Example:
1. My thighs
2. My sometimes-too-sharp-of-words
3. My impatience.

Now sit with those things a bit. Think about HOW HAVE THEY SERVED YOU at some point.

Example:
1. They made me sturdy as a rock
2. They made people think
3. I made shit happen.

We don't have to be scared of what we hate. In fact, when we sit in the ICK, and look at something that you've avoided or ignored for a while, we can gain respect for it.

Things you dislike:

1.
2.
3.

How these things have served you at some point:

1.
2.
3.

**THIS PROTECTED ME
WHEN I NEEDED TO BE A WARRIOR.**

KNOW

The release:

Step 1:
It is dark and rainy, it's not something you want to look at. You can't see it well, but it feels heavy. It feels dark.

Step 2:
The sun shows us new angles we didn't see before, and beauty can shine through. We see it in a new light and we choose to see how it served us.

Step 3:
The perspective shift allows the weight to shift. we are no longer burdened because the weight of it all was all in our head, the darkness is what made it so heavy. We can now blow it away.

KNOW

be at peace
know you are okay
get outside
      smile
      laugh
      tip well

be a good human[*]

be nice to your soul

it is soft &
changing &
      trying

love love love every part of you &
      give yourself grace

so that you can give grace to others around you

---

[*] hello, FB group! xo

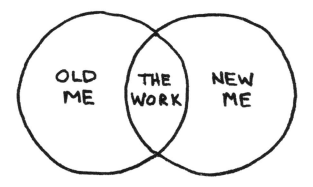

KNOW

waiting to open the new door
wondering why it won't open[*]

---

[*] You can't shut the old door and you can't open the new door for a reason.

KNOW

I grew
I grew
I grew

Now all I want to do is hibernate.

(why is growth so fucking exhausting)

KNOW

raw skin
exposed for the first time
like my ripped palm
wishing for the callous to form
burning with every drop of sweat
staring at it like watching water boil
knowing it would take so much time before I could
    grip without grimace

now I look at my hands
as if they were always this way

no wonder babies always sleep.

KNOW

I am a force
Disguised in messy bun hair
Lost keys
And missing forks

I am a genius
With toes turned in
Patience as short as a blade of grass
Looking up and wishing sometimes I was more graceful
Like a daisy or a tree
But knowing I can be those too

I am XX
Brave
Unwavering
Waiting patiently with a smile
For the world to nod back the way I have nodded at it

I write like my body moves best
Eyes closed
Trying to experience and feel and breathe through every step
Because when I open my eyes I think
I think like wildfire moves in dry season
Brain on fire as fast as that match is lit
And that's part of the mess but part of the magic

I am unstoppable
Because I know I'm unstoppable and the people who know it too
Didn't need me to tell them

KNOW

Pull your shoulders back
Look them in the eye
Firm shake and fuck it if it's too firm
Make them notice

You were nothing but on this earth to be noticed
Strip the layers
Strip the doubt
Insecurity has no place in your bones
It's not at home there
It's a transplant
And you don't need it to clothe you

Strip it off
Breathe it out
Click those heels together

Come back home to your body.

WHAT WOULD IT LOOK LIKE if you lived in a world with nothing to fear?

Out of curiosity, I googled most common fears and what came up were the things like public speaking, spiders, or heights. While I don't disagree that these are extremely real fears, I was disappointed that the most common fears I see in myself and in others are not labeled fears at all. They are called "stressors."

But stressors are just that: fears manifested.

KNOW

> We stress about things we don't know the answer to,
> the things we can't control
> and then we stress about the stress
> Only digging a deeper hole

We sit at the bottom of this hole, confused at how the hell we got there, too afraid to climb out of it because fear is why we are there in the first place.

When there is fear in our life, there is stress. When there is stress in our life, there is fear.

I went to my tribe of good humans and asked them to help me pinpoint their biggest stressors, the biggest fears. It was very clear there were two that resounded the most for my people:

#1: body image
#2: money and finances

They also happen to be the two that I've battled the most in my life.

> Puking in the bathroom.
> Running and running and running.
> Wishing I could cut off my mermaid thighs.
> Not able to look in the mirror.
> Avoiding my bank account.
> Terrified of debt.
> Thinking money was evil.
> Feeling guilty for making money.
> Creating worst case scenario after worst case scenarios.
> Obsessively checking my bank account.
> Unsure of how the fuck I was going to pull it off.

KNOW

The very root of our existence is feeling safe in our body and making sure we feel secure in our home. It took a very long time to change both of these, but it is not only possible, it is a necessity for absolutely anything good you want to get out of life.

First we look at the stress, then we ask:
What is the fear around this stress?

Stressor = my body
What is the fear around my stress of my body?
Fear =
For me it was the fear that what I saw in the mirror was not who I was. That I wasn't good enough as is and that I was flawed by looking different. My body didn't match my own expectations, and it left me walking in life with an awareness that only I could see but was all-consuming, changing the way I showed up in the world.

Stressor = money
What is the fear around my stress of money?
Fear =
For me it was the fear that I bit off more than I could chew. That I was going to prove the wrong people right, and the right people wrong. That I would fail. That I created, then I had to fund it, then I kept creating to keep funding it, and the cycle never ends leaving me holding my breath wondering if I would be better off locked in a closet so I would stop creating things.

KNOW

Fill in the blank:

Stressor =
What is the fear around it?

Stressor =
What is the fear around it?

Stressor =
What is the fear around it?

Stressor =
What is the fear around it?

Stressor =
What is the fear around it?

KNOW

did they teach you it wasn't a good thing
        that it only caused problems
        and it was called GREED

did they teach you it can't be desired
        to just use on necessities
        or on the mouths that you feed

did they teach you there is only so much to go around
        that **less** keeps you humble
        and **more** is like a weed

a man once tried to take my wallet..
he almost got away with it

                                    but I stopped him.

KNOW

I am coming back home to my body.
I am coming back home to my body.
I am coming back home to my body.

my heart got cracked open this week
like my best friend
eating an egg on a sandwich
for the first time
She didn't know the
egg yolk would run like it did
Her face of terror
As yellow ran down her arm
felt like my week of rest
Discomfort, strange, out of body
That's when things come to light
When things unbind
A foreign sense of freedom
Although uncomfortable
Is the right thing surfacing
After the surprise in the gasp
Your new favorite sandwich
simply waiting for you to step back
And let the egg crack

KNOW

When you choose to look the darkest parts of you right in the eye
No fear
No hesitation
Not even a blink...

The world becomes your exhale

KNOW

How can you stop to smell the flowers when this is all you see?

This "spiral out of control when basic needs aren't being met" is all too real for me.

What originally started in my journey as my body and my skin pivoted effortlessly into my business and my creations:

How do I look
How big is this pimple
How crooked are my teeth
How is my cellulite

KNOW

to:

How am I going to pay for inventory
How am I going to pull off this launch
How am I going to hire the person I need to help this grow
HOW THE FUCK AM I GOING TO DO THIS

The fears we have are not made up. They are very real, and very primal.

When we have needs not being met, whether actual or imagined, it tells your body one thing:

I am not safe here.

90% of health issues, from digestive woes to adrenal dysfunction to inflammation to weight gain, are caused by STRESS. I argue 88% of our health issues stem from the fact that we are not taught to
KNOW
TRUST
LOVE
BELIEVE
in our own damn selves.

Remember this line, my OGs?
BE YOUR OWN SUPERHERO.

For me that was looking at people doing really rad things realizing I was slowly separating myself from them.

They did something hard, there was no way I could do that. I wanted it more than anything but the BELIEF WAS NOT THERE.

What we look for we will find.
What we expect we will get.

That goes for the negative and for the positive.

> Hard things are happening to me – I am worried about these hard things – I need to problem-solve them and focus on them – this is not looking good – I must prepare for the worst – I am now expecting the worst and finding the worst – what I expected is happening – I SEE NOTHING POSITIVE – the worst is occurring – I am in the hole – deep in the hole

This hole becomes an island that only you are on, and despite all the glorious dreams you once had and the motivation that was so brightly lit, here we are simply surviving on the island alone.

There is no easy way to stop seeing the tunnel, and it's a long boat ride to get away from the island.

> Finally start to accept my body → try on jeans → FUCK EVERYONE
> Finally feel better about my skin → see mirror → I LOOK LIKE A MOP
> Finally work out because it feels good → weigh oneself → I WANT TO DIE
> Finally feel great about my business → bad month of sales → CHANGE EVERYTHING IMMEDIATELY

There are triggers all around us.
It is amplified by comparison.
But we keep doing the work by noticing it and telling it hello.

TRIGGERS ⟶ SCALES
MIRRORS
JEANS
SALES

COMPARISON ⟶ SOCIAL MEDIA

THE WORK ⟶ KNOW YOURSELF
TRUST YOURSELF
LOVE YOURSELF
BELIEVE IN YOURSELF

The work helps us trust that every time there is a trigger, we don't expect it to be gone. We expect it to be smaller.

KNOW

Finally start to accept my body → try on jeans → FUCK EVERYONE
Finally feel better about my skin → see mirror → I LOOK LIKE A MOP
Finally work out because it feels good → weigh oneself → I WANT TO DIE
Finally feel great about my business → bad month of sales → CHANGE EVERYTHING IMMEDIATELY

Finally start to accept my body → try on jeans → FUCK EVERYONE
Finally feel better about my skin → see mirror → I LOOK LIKE A MOP
Finally work out because it feels good → weigh oneself → I WANT TO DIE
Finally feel great about my business → bad month of sales → CHANGE EVERYTHING IMMEDIATELY

Finally start to accept my body → try on jeans → fuck everyone
Finally feel better about my skin → see mirror → I look like a mop
Finally work out because it feels good → weigh oneself → I want to die
Finally feel great about my business → bad month of sales → change everything immediately

KNOW

Your "bottom"
the point that you think you've hit when the trigger clicks
it hits you so hard
you tap out
        not because you lack motivation
        or the know-how
        or the desire

But because it feels like ground zero
                why try so hard
                      care so much
                            give this much effort
If there isn't even a little give

Your "bottom" IS NO LONGER THE STARTING POINT.
        You are not regressing.
                It is not as bad as you think.
                      Give yourself more credit,
                                you just can't see your growth.

KNOW

Too much feeling = crazy brain
Too much doing = crazy brain
Too little of knowing = crazy brain

How to get out of the crazy brain:

```
        Crazy brain
            ↓
         FEEL.  →  if feeling isn't
                      working
                        ↓
  if doing isn't  ←    DO.
     working
        ↓
     work on the
        KNOW.
```

MAKE

MAKE

CREATE FROM LOVE CREATE FROM LOVE CREATE FROM LOVE[*]

---

[*] Fuck this is hard

Someone once told me you can't create from fear.
I called bullshit.

> I had bills to pay.
> I had rent to make.
> I had to figure out how to stop defaulting my bank account.

There is a healthy amount of fear we all have when we start. If someone says otherwise, don't be afraid to call them on their bullshit, too.

The problem is… We stay stuck in that fear.

The work is understanding that one day you will hit a point where **fear will be your limiting factor.**

MAKE

#phasesoftheentrepreneur

MAKE

I have this weird thing with boiling eggs
I refuse to use a timer
        And they are perfect every time

Any time I doubt my intuition
I boil some eggs

MAKE

when will you stop being busy

                                            so
                                      damn
                                      busy

filling every space with all that it can hold
and then adding a little more
because no one said "stop"

lines bursting right at the seams
lines we weren't afraid to cross
       because we created them
       so we fill them
and then add a little more
       which makes us brave
       but also broken

over the top and on to the ground
       this is no longer a cup overflowing
       it is a DOWNPOUR
       and it isn't slowing down

as you start to get cold
       you pile on more clothes
standing soaking wet
       from your head to your toes

when your body starts to shiver
       you drown out the sound
when your hands turn into raisins
       you turn them around

and it is only when your soul feels heavy

                                      so
                                  damn
                                  heavy
                drenched, from the outside-in

that you start to notice
"I've been in the flood for too long"

MAKE

       want to rest
       runaway
       leave

               what would it feel like to EXHALE

MAKE

THINK BIGGER, EMILY.

Do I not think big because I don't think I can?

MAKE

Who do you want to be in 6 months:

Creative
Free
Happy.
not
resentful
Brave.
bold

~~Why does this even matter when that person doesn't exist inside.~~

MAKE

breathe it in
    breathe it out
        be proud
        be gentle
        be nice

compassion has to come from deep inside of you
    (and to you)
before it can extend to others

        You will always be able to figure it out.

MAKE

      on this stage
      always a dream
      the battle was understanding
      if I was worthy of it
           because we live in a world
           where we aren't worthy
      you fight every demon
      wishing to live
      until you suddenly realize

                    those who are truly
                          l i v i n g
                    aren't worried about being
                          w o r t h y

MAKE

The energy pulled
    & given
    & taken
    & received
    & given

    This is the cycle of business.

MAKE

This isn't another poem about listening to your body
Or how I won't feel guilty about not doing XYZ
Those are actions and while important
It's the unspoken feeling of respect
Knowing your power
relishing in it
(humbly)
walking in it
(proudly)
And not needing to explain anything you do to anyone
Because there is nothing to prove anymore
And there never was

How many people have
to believe in you
before you believe in yourself?

MAKE

My heart is full because I know everything will be okay
No matter what
I visualize every brick
The espresso machine
The overwhelming amount of green
Persist
Push
Hang on
Never hear them
Go go go

MAKE

White-knuckled
We grip on to what once soared from us and through us
our words our art our sound
muddied with fear
now the
damaged wing
the crack in the voice
the hue that just doesn't sit on the canvas quite right

        and we wonder why our inspiration left us

once so brave
the paradox of bringing something into this world
out of desire and fate
screaming into existence
as if there ever was a choice
now consumed by numbers
stats
likes
views
sales

        and we wonder why we feel all of it is pointless

the constant seeking
uncovering layers at exactly the right moment
almost too late
but in perfect harmony
for when we are actually ready
to hear it
to feel it
to digest it
exactly as we need to

        and we wonder why we feel so much

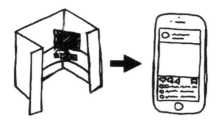

We live our life in these scrolling boxes
Digital cubicles
Before the 9 and way past the 5
Filtered
Strategic
All-consuming
Inherently flawed by being solely one dimensional
Taunting us to let go of the depth of our oceans
Layer by layer
Until we are drowning in nothing more
Than a puddle

MAKE

I CAN WISH FOR MORE AND NOT LOSE DEPTH.
I CAN WISH FOR MORE AND NOT LOSE DEPTH.
I CAN WISH FOR MORE AND NOT LOSE DEPTH.

MAKE

VS.

More depth requires more time, more effort, more intention.

Maybe demanding more depth is as simple as asking:

"what is the intention?"

MAKE

There's only so much room.

I love who I am becoming
I love who I am becoming
I love who I am becoming
I love who I am becoming
I've been waiting for her for so long

MAKE

MAKE

whatever ball in my hand had the focus
sometimes one, sometimes two
a brief moment of focus
before suspended again
constant movement
    catch
    release
    catch
    release

        one mis-timed moment
            would end it all

I created each ball
I brought them to life
I chose them as much as they chose me

what if
what if
what if
I can stop the juggling
    (I'm getting tired of juggling)

and if they drop,
    that's ok

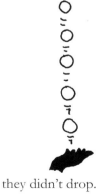

they didn't drop.

MAKE

~~YOU~~
↓
an incredible life force that moves through you and uses you
because you are willing to receive

↓

you

↓

them

MAKE

When you live your truth
It scares everyone who isn't
That's the problem with growth
Although it's not really a problem
Because you are living
And they are dying
Even with a death sentence on the same day

Shy away
Caged bird
You'll be next to fly

MAKE

overwhelmed
but feeling more optimistic

it is long
it is lonely
it is harder than I thought
      not the fixing
      and the doing

but the **constant** of the fixing and doing

that is when things get heavy:
      the less you can come up for air

so I choose to store store store my air
and dive dive dive

I AM CAPABLE OF THIS

MAKE

MAKE

NOISE < VIBRATION

MAKE

Did you know there is a type of whale that can vibrate you
    to death
It is at a frequency at which humans cannot hear
Only feel

We talk
We yell
We scream
And then wonder if they are deaf

You can only be heard when they are ready to listen
And if they won't hear you?

                        MOVE THEM.

MAKE

(the identity crisis)

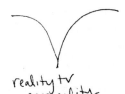

Identity:
    passions
    labels
    things you care about
    what the world sees you as
    what you want the world to see you as
    comfort blankets
    things that will change at some point in your life
        because we are meant to evolve

MAKE

GIVE YOURSELF PERMISSION TO PART WAYS.

Stop chasing the old you…
Maybe it is time for something new

MAKE

I used to love tomatoes
Now I hate them
I don't judge myself for hating tomatoes

Give yourself room to be a different you
Maybe something in you knows it could be better
or it just doesn't fit like it used to

Your world is a canvas
Make it whatever you want
        And when you want it to be different
        Start it all over again

MAKE

You can't create flow
As if it's a human right
   Or something to be summoned

When it comes over you
you just jump
unafraid to stop everything
and let her swallow you whole

If those moments call
And you ignore them
(Or save them for later like another open tab)

You tell your intuition you are too busy
and then beg for her to come back
looking in all the wrong places and people
       eyes on too many screens
       head heavy
       soul drained

As she waits for you patiently in the smell of the pine trees
And the rush of the river
Under the bright sun
And in between your barefoot toes

MAKE

Looking for each other
Needing each other
The chances of collision more and more slim
as we separate from the beauty
              the art
              the freedom
              of creation

Choosing strings
    attachments
    safe stories
    instead

Flow is not a guarantee
Or promise

It is a gift
Listen to her when she arrives

MAKE

It all feels so light when things are going well.

MAKE

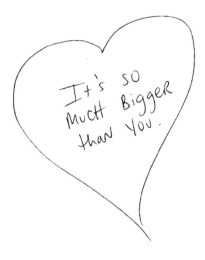

MAKE

TODAY's TO-DO LIST:
stay calm
stay focused
tru_s_t the process
eat good food
drink enough water
laugh ≤ <u>3x</u>.

MAKE

MAKE

It was a WTF kind of day.

MAKE

It was a
WTF
kind of
day

MAKE

We did not
do it
grow it
create it

But without us, there would be nothing

MAKE

We take credit,
therefore we take responsibility

        If we release ownership
        We release our incessant need for control.*

---

*more lessons from my garden

MAKE

> For a second I thought I could chill
>   (which allowed me to chill)
> And then I realized…
>
>   It's about to begin.

MAKE

What you "want" journey

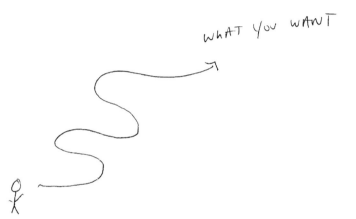

Stop looking left or right just look step to step

MAKE

LiFE is:
        hard
        simple
        easy
        hard
        beautiful
        hard
        simple
        easy
        easy
        hard
        hard
        hard
        hard
        easy
        BEAUTIFUL.

be more accessible ⟶

⟶ <u>be more visible</u>.

Why does this
terrify me?

↙ ↓ ↘
FEAR   DISLIKE   I'M NOT MYSELF

MAKE

WORTH	SELF-CARE
FOCUS	GROWTH

Entrepreneurship for Empaths 1-0-1

Worth:
    Fix your relationship with money. As soon as possible.

Focus:
    Commit to the things that energize you, avoiding the things you think you "should be doing".*

Self-Care:
    Separating SELF from work: what we do is an extension of who we are, but who we are is not what we do

Growth:
    Growing a business in your own, unique way. (not the way you assume you should because it's worked for someone else.)

---

see page 103

MAKE

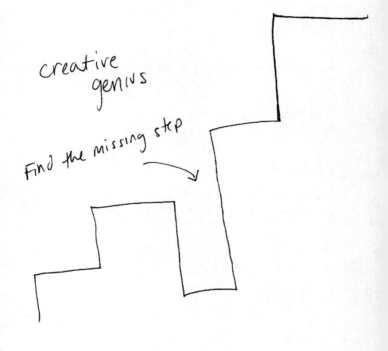

on flow

the dilemma:

    is this hard because it's inconvenient or is this hard because I need to let it go

the question:

    if it was going perfectly, would I be obsessed with it?

the solution:

    choose to fight or choose to let go or you'll drive yourself mad
    (you'll know soon enough if you need to pivot)

the process of a new idea #1:

extremely excited
    you tell someone your idea
        they don't match your excitement
            you care a little less

the process of a new idea #2:

thrilled but nervous
    immediately talk yourself out of it
        think about it for a long, long time
            wish you would have done it (and still might)

the process of a new idea #3:

unsure of what it means
    digs into it a little bit more
        someone else has done it better
            moves on

the process of a new idea #4:

completely consumed
    starts to bring it to life
        constant battle between euphoria and
            "this is dumb"

the process of a new idea #5:

try it the way you think it should be done
    it doesn't work, realize it's all wrong
        let go of expectations of how it should be done
            it begins to work out perfectly

                Remember: we are simply gardeners.

MAKE

blessed
as if it was some beautiful accident
waiting for the moment it all disappears

lucky
as if the sweat on our brow and the burden we carry
is heavy but not heavy enough

guilty
because how could it be this good
when there is so much bad all around me

undeserving
because while we are too busy serving
everyone else is worth it
       except us
       not me
       I don't deserve that

My mom always told me
"the universe is aligned for you"
               and I choose to not fight it any more.

I hope that you learn to create without expectation because the expectations will be the only limit.

MAKE

Infinity
n.
in·fin·i·ty | \ in-ˈfi-nə-tē
the moment we see ourselves as creators

OUTRO

The process of . . .

Real World DC → hated what I saw on TV

EMFIT

→ Moved to CO to run away from it all

didn't work, got worse ←

got sick of my own shit → Joined a rec center →

Couldn't jump rope for 60 seconds

felt like a superhero everytime I left the gym ← Kept showing up

↓ knew I could help other people do that too → moved to Denver to become a trainer →

Washed dogs for money

hated working for other people ← finally got hired as a trainer ← worked the front desk

↓ quit → Unleashed Fitness LLC → rebranded to EMFIT

my Emfit online programs were "dumbbell only" → client needed heavier dumbbells

stuffed my suitcase with everything ← I was traveling a lot, always disappointed with hotel gyms

had an idea → found the right people → launched the idea to Kickstarter

fully funded in DAY ONE ←

Started the process of creating the first & only backpack turned weight-training bag

EVOLVED/MOTION

ELEMENT

- Now had 2 businesses
- was competing in CrossFit
- drove myself into the ground
- Needed to cut caffeine
- realized how miserable life was without coffee
- played around with coffee alternatives
- hated them
- created Herbal Coffee
- became happy again
- started studying herbal medicine
- made Xmas presents out of new tea blends
- they were a hit
- Made 5 official herbal tea remedies

- knew it was time to move my business online
- → missed people + conversations
- → hated working solo
- → needed good people + conversations
- → started a podcast "Emfit Radio"
- → hated the name
- → asked Bradford to explain me in 2 words
- → "Meathead Hippie"
- → instantly rebranded

MEATHEAD HIPPIE ≫→

wanted to do a deep dive into topics that changed my life

→ **the body awareness project**

↓

acne

↓

adrenal dysfunction

↓

gut issues

← wanted to collab with experts

↓

wanted to create an experience of healing

→ online course

↓

add a box of essentials

↓

The Body Awareness Project
→ skin
→ adrenals
→ gut + digestion

Total meathead who quit CrossFit → joined globo-gym

↓

got sick of headphones + gyms closed on Sundays

← decided it was time for a home base

↓

incredible programming

→ individualized →

PLATFORM STRENGTH

Platform Strength

about the author

EMILY SCHROMM IS A TRAINER, coach, Nutritional Therapy Practitioner, and entrepreneur. From reality tv to *Women's Health Magazine*'s Next Fitness Star, Emily has worked in the industry for over 8 years helping people learn about movement, mindset, and the power of nutrition.

She is the founder of EmFit, which provides online 21-day challenges and 6-week strength programs to help people learn about their body and feel stronger than ever at any level. @emfitchallenge

She is the Founder of Evolved Motion, the home of the #empack. The world's first and only backpack turned weight training bag, helping you stay strong at home or on-the-go. @evolvedmotion

She is the Founder of Herbal Element, an herbal tea company with blends to help with digestion, anxiety, stress, and hormones. @herbalelement

She is the Founder of The Body Awareness Project, an educational course + box of essentials on three of the most relevant topics in today's world covering acne, stress, sleep, and bloating. @bodyawarenessproject

She is the Founder of Platform Strength, a 24/7-access gym in RiNO, Denver, providing group classes and personal training. @platformstrength

She is the Founder of MYEMPIRICA, a pharmaceutical-grade supplement company providing the highest quality nutrients in our nutrient-lacking diet to support our system. @myempirica

She is the Founder of EMPRESS, a monthly digital publication that connects people to information outside of typical media coverage, delivering information and education in an interactive way.

She is the host of the Meathead Hippie® Podcast.

And now, because of you, she is an author.

Thank you for being here.

of Metro Denver

$1 of every book goes to Girls Inc of Metro Denver
girlsincdenver.com

Made in the USA
Middletown, DE
31 December 2019